HOW DO WE LIVE TOGETHER?
RACCOONS

BY LUCIA RAATMA

COMMUNITY · CONNECTIONS

CHERRY LAKE Publishing

Published in the United States of America by Cherry Lake Publishing
Ann Arbor, Michigan
www.cherrylakepublishing.com

Content Adviser: Stephen S. Ditchkoff, PhD, Associate Professor, School of Forestry and
Wildlife Sciences, Auburn University
Reading Adviser: Cecilia Minden-Cupp, PhD, Literacy Consultant

Photo Credits: Cover and page 1, ©Xavier MARCHANT, used under license from Shutterstock,
Inc.; page 5, ©Scott Camazine/PHOTOTAKE/Alamy; page 7, ©Infomages, used under license
from Shutterstock, Inc.; page 9, ©iStockphoto.com/kawisign; page 11, ©iStockphoto.com/
HansUntch; page 13, ©iStockphoto.com/EEI_Tony; page 15, ©:: IntraClique :: LLC, used under
license from Shutterstock, Inc.; page 17, ©Utekhina Anna, used under license from Shutterstock,
Inc.; page 19, ©iStockphoto.com/Lupico; page 21, ©iStockphoto.com/cullenphotos

LIBRARY OF CONGRESS CATALOGING-IN-PUBLICATION DATA
Raatma, Lucia.
  How do we live together? Raccoons / by Lucia Raatma.
    p. cm.—(Community connections)
  Includes bibliographical references and index.
  ISBN-13: 978-1-60279-619-5
  ISBN-10: 1-60279-619-X
  1. Raccoon—Juvenile literature. I. Title. II. Title: Raccoons.
III. Series.
  QL737.C26R33 2010
  599.76'32—dc22   2009023402

Cherry Lake Publishing would like to acknowledge the
work of The Partnership for 21st Century Skills. Please
visit www.21stcenturyskills.org for more information.

Printed in the United States of America
Corporate Graphics Inc.
January 2010
CLSP06

RACCOONS

CONTENTS

4 **Who's in the Garbage?**

10 **A Closer Look at Raccoons**

16 **Sharing the Great Outdoors**

22 Glossary

23 Find Out More

24 Index

24 About the Author

HOW DO WE LIVE TOGETHER?

WHO'S IN THE GARBAGE?

Crash! You hear your trash can fall over. You look outside. The trash can lid is rolling down the driveway. Trash is everywhere. A small, dark animal is digging through pizza boxes. Who's in the garbage?

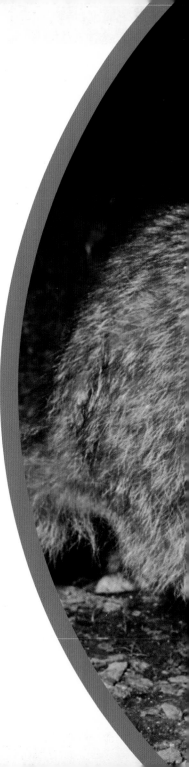

Raccoons often raid garbage cans for tasty treats.

It's a raccoon! These **mammals** like to get into your garbage. They are looking for food. They can leave a mess. Many neighborhoods have everything raccoons need. That's why raccoons are often found in towns. They can survive far away from their natural **habitats**.

Have you ever seen raccoons in your neighborhood?

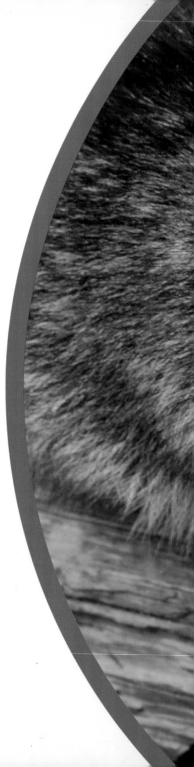

Many people see raccoons as pests. They may be cute, but they are wild animals. They can carry diseases. They can also cause damage to homes.

Raccoons still have a right to use the outdoors. They need shelter and food, just like you. Humans and raccoons need to find ways to get along.

All wild animals need a place to live.

Do you want to know more about raccoons? Maybe you want to learn ways to stay safe around them. Talk to someone at your local zoo or wildlife department. Animal experts will be happy to answer your questions.

A CLOSER LOOK AT RACCOONS

Have you ever seen a raccoon? The first thing you notice is the dark fur around its eyes. This "mask" is one reason raccoons are known for mischief.

Raccoons also have bushy tails with dark rings. They live throughout North America and in parts of Europe and Japan.

Do you see the furry mask on this raccoon?

Usually raccoons live in forests, grasslands, and marshes. Raccoons live in **dens**. These dens can be anything from logs to caves!

In the wild, raccoons often eat fish. They also like insects and other small animals. They eat fruit and nuts, too. In **urban** areas, raccoons will eat just about anything.

Urban raccoons might even steal cat food!

Raccoons are **nocturnal**. This means they are most active at night. When you are camping, you might hear something moving outside. It could be a raccoon. Raccoons will go through almost anything. They are looking for food. A hungry raccoon is very determined!

Raccoons can see in the dark.

MAKE A GUESS!

Do you think raccoons are afraid of other animals? If you said yes, you are right. Coyotes and dogs hunt raccoons. Bobcats and cougars do, too. People also hunt and trap them.

SHARING THE GREAT OUTDOORS

Imagine if you found a raccoon in your basement. Would you be scared? What if you had to clean up garbage that a raccoon had scattered in your yard? You would probably be upset. So how can we get along with raccoons?

It can be scary to meet a raccoon up close!

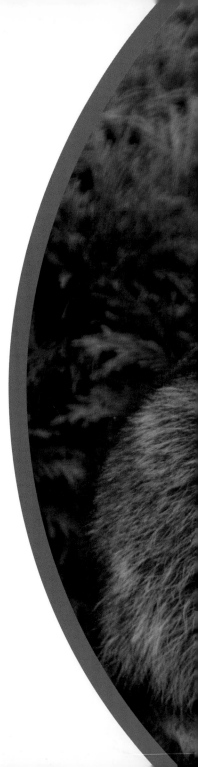

One way to deal with raccoons is to be sure your trash can has a tight-fitting lid. You can also block holes in your house. That way raccoons cannot get inside.

What if a raccoon does get in your house? You should get an adult right away. The raccoon will attack if you corner it.

Many raccoons can open garbage cans.

Keep your pets inside at night. Feed them inside, too. Raccoons can carry diseases, including **rabies**. You do not want your pet to get in a fight with a raccoon.

Raccoons are smart and interesting animals. We must find ways to respect their needs. There is room in the world for all of us!

Raccoons are an important part of the world around us.

LOOK!

Look around your neighborhood. Is there food out where raccoons can get it? Are there holes where raccoons could enter your home? Paying attention to these things can prevent raccoons from causing trouble.

GLOSSARY

dens (DENZ) homes for wild animals, including raccoons

habitats (HAB-uh-tatss) the places and natural conditions in which plants and animals live

mammals (MAM-uhlz) warm-blooded animals that are usually covered in hair, have backbones, give birth to live young, and make milk to feed their babies

nocturnal (nok-TUR-nuhl) active at night

rabies (RAY-beez) a dangerous disease that is spread by animals that already have it

urban (UR-buhn) having to do with a city or living in a city

FIND OUT MORE

BOOKS

Hurtig, Jennifer. *Raccoons*. New York: Weigl Publishers, 2008.

Ripple, William John. *Raccoons*. Mankato, MN: Pebble Books, 2006.

WEB SITES

Animal Planet—Raccoon
animal.discovery.com/mammals/raccoon/
Learn more about raccoons and how they live.

National Geographic Society—Raccoon
animals.nationalgeographic.com/animals/mammals/raccoon.html
Get more information about raccoons and their habits.

INDEX

animal experts, 9

bobcats, 15

cougars, 15
coyotes, 15

dens, 12
diseases, 8, 20
dogs, 15

eyes, 10

fish, 12
foods, 6, 8, 12,
   14, 21
fruits, 12
fur, 10

garbage, 4, 6,
   16, 18

habitats, 6, 10, 12
houses, 8, 18,
   21

insects, 12

mammals, 6
masks, 10

nocturnal animals,
   14
nuts, 12

people, 8, 15
pests, 8
pets, 20

rabies, 20

tails, 10

urban areas, 6, 12

ABOUT THE AUTHOR

Lucia Raatma has written dozens of books for young readers. She and her family live in the Tampa Bay area of Florida. A raccoon once got into their house through a broken screen!